Fun
and
Easy
Things
to Make

(*Original title*: Beginning Crafts for Beginning Readers)

by ALICE GILBREATH

Pictures by JOE ROGERS

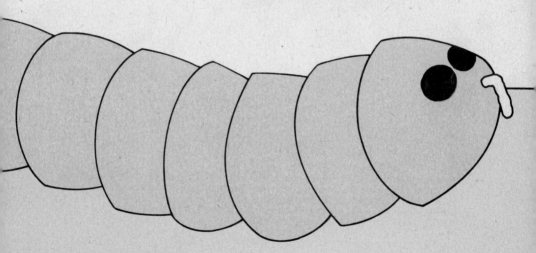

SCHOLASTIC INC.
NEW YORK · TORONTO · LONDON · AUCKLAND · SYDNEY · TOKYO

ISBN 0-590-04837-6

"Picture Magnets" copyright 1966. First published in *Wee Wisdom*. Text copyright © 1972 by Alice Gilbreath. Illustrations copyright © 1972 by Follett Publishing Company, a division of Follett Corporation. All rights reserved. This edition is published by Scholastic Inc., 730 Broadway, New York, NY 10003, by arrangement with Follett Publishing Company, publishers of the book under the title BEGINNING CRAFTS FOR BEGINNING READERS.

20 19 18 17 16 15 14 13 12 11 10   3 4 5 6 7/8

To
my husband, Rex,
my children, Rex, Jr. and Sue,
and my sister, Margaret

Totem Pole

To make a totem pole, you will need these things:

three wooden spools

three gum wrappers

black and red poster paint

a paintbrush

glue

When you have all these things, follow these steps:

1. Put glue on top of one spool.
   Put another spool on
   top of the glue.
   Now you have two spools
   glued together.

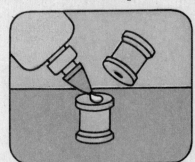

2. Put glue on the top spool.
   Put the third spool
   on the glue.
   Now you have three
   spools glued together.
   Let the glue dry.

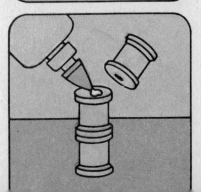

3. With your paintbrush,
   paint one side of each
   gum wrapper black.
   Wash your paintbrush.
   Let the paint dry.

4. With your paintbrush,
   paint the spools red.
   Paint red faces on the
   black gum wrappers.
   Let the paint dry.

5. Put a dot of glue on
   the front of each spool.
   Put the back of the gum
   wrapper faces on the glue.
   Put one face on
   the top spool.
   Put one face on
   the middle spool.
   Put one face on
   the bottom spool.

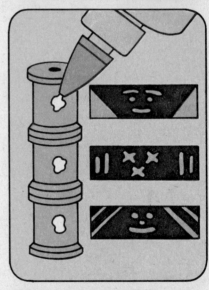

6 Your totem pole is done.
   Make another totem pole
   for a friend and put
   different faces on it.

Locket

To make a locket, you will need these things:

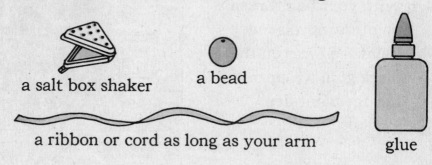

a salt box shaker   a bead

a ribbon or cord as long as your arm   glue

When you have all these things, follow these steps:

1. Tie the ends of the ribbon or cord together.

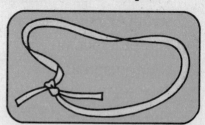

2. Open the salt box shaker. Put the center of the ribbon or cord inside the shaker.

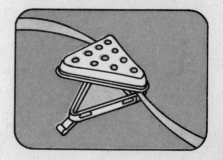

3. Close the shaker.

4. Put glue on top
    of the shaker.
    Put the bead
    on the glue.
    Let the glue dry.

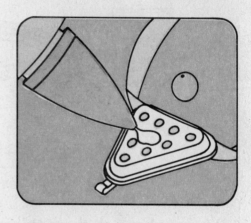

5. Your locket is done.
    Put a picture inside
    it if you wish.
    Wear your locket
    around your neck.
    You might want to
    make another locket
    for a friend.

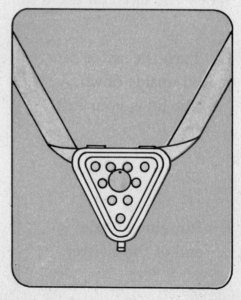

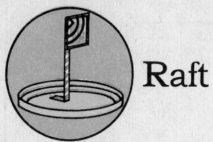

Raft

To make a raft, you will need these things:

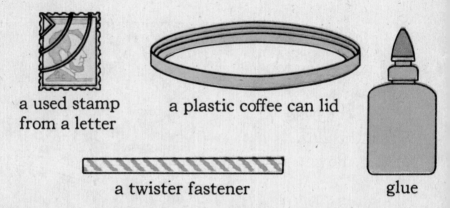

a used stamp
from a letter

a plastic coffee can lid

a twister fastener

glue

When you have all these things, follow these steps:

1. Turn the coffee can
   lid upside down.
   The lid is your raft.

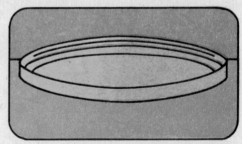

2. Put glue on one
   end of the twister.

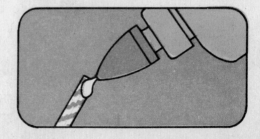

3. Put one edge of the
   stamp on the glue.
   This is the flag
   for your raft.

4. Bend the bottom part
   of the twister.
   Make the bent part
   as wide as two
   of your fingers.

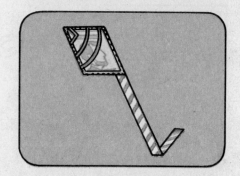

5. Put glue in the center
   of your raft.
   Put the bent part of
   the twister in the glue.
   Let the glue dry.
   Now the flag will
   stand up.

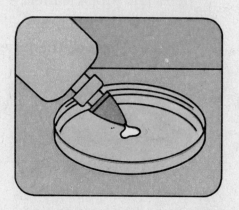

6. Your raft is done.
   Put it in water.
   Blow on the raft
   to make it move.

Puppet

To make a puppet, you will need these things:

a picture of
a boy or a girl

scissors

a pipe cleaner

glue

When you have all these things, follow these steps:

1. With your fingers,
   bend the pipe cleaner.
   Bend it in the center.
   The two ends of the pipe
   cleaner are the legs
   of the puppet.

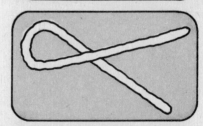

2. Shape the center of the
   pipe cleaner into a circle.
   Make the circle big
   enough so you can put
   your finger through it.

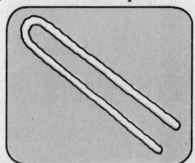

3. Cross the legs at the
   bottom of the circle.
   Twist one leg all the way
   around the other leg.

4. Bend the pipe cleaner circle halfway down.

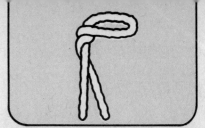

5. With your scissors, cut out the picture of a boy or girl.
If the picture of the boy or girl has legs, cut them off.

6. Put glue on the top part of the puppet's legs.
Put the center of the boy or girl on the glue.
Let the glue dry.

7. Your puppet is done. Put your finger in the pipe cleaner circle. Move your finger to make your puppet walk. You can have a puppet play if you make other puppets of men, women, and animals.

Butterfly Bookmark

To make a butterfly bookmark, you will need these things:

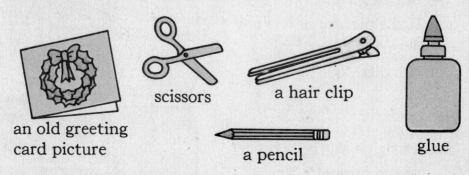

an old greeting
card picture

scissors

a hair clip

a pencil

glue

When you have these things, follow these steps:

1. Fold the greeting card
   picture in half.
   Put the fold near you.

2. Put your fingers together,
   but not your thumb.
   Put them on the fold
   of the greeting card.
   With a pencil, draw
   around your fingers.

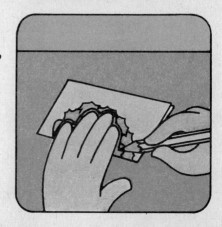

14

3. With scissors, cut both halves of the card along the line you drew.

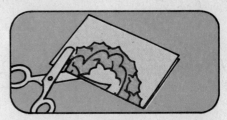

4. Cut off both corners of the card.
Unfold the card.
It looks like a butterfly.

5. Put glue down the center of the butterfly.

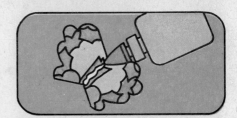

6. Open the hair clip.
Clip it on the center of the butterfly.
The hair clip is the butterfly's body.

7. Your butterfly is a bookmark.
Clip your butterfly to the top of a page.
The butterfly will keep your place in a book.

Firecracker Bank

To make a firecracker bank, you will need these things:

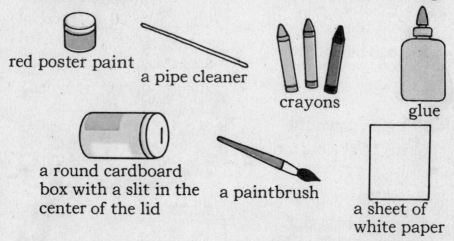

red poster paint

a pipe cleaner

crayons

glue

a round cardboard
box with a slit in the
center of the lid

a paintbrush

a sheet of
white paper

When you have all these things, follow these steps:

1. With your paintbrush,
    paint the box red.
    Let the paint dry.

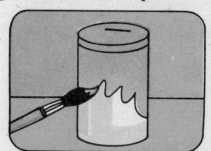

2. With crayons, draw eyes,
    nose, and mouth
    on the white paper.

3. With the scissors,
   cut out the eyes,
   nose, and mouth.

4. Glue the eyes, nose, and
   mouth on the box.

5. With your fingers, bend
   one end of the pipe cleaner.
   Bend it into a little circle.

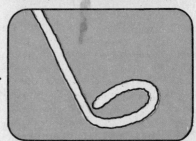

6. Glue the pipe cleaner circle
   on top of the firecracker.

7. Your firecracker bank
   is done.
   Put coins through
   the slit in the lid.

17

Vase of Flowers

To make a vase of flowers, you will need these things:

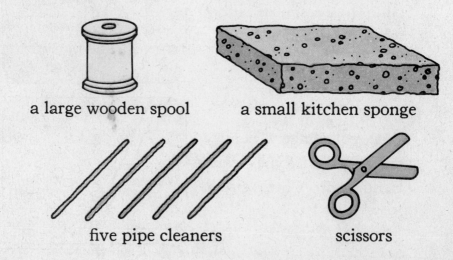

a large wooden spool   a small kitchen sponge

five pipe cleaners   scissors

After you have all these things, follow these steps:

1. With your scissors, cut
    a sponge into five squares.
    The pieces of sponge
    are your flowers.

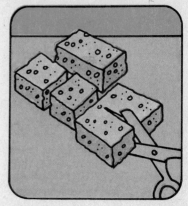

2. Hold one flower in
   your hand.
   Put the end of one pipe
   cleaner through the
   center of the flower.
   The pipe cleaner is
   the stem of the flower.

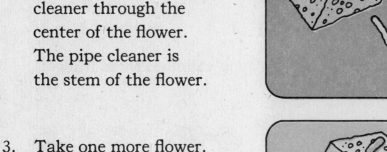

3. Take one more flower.
   Take one more stem.
   Put the stem through
   the center of the flower.

4. Make three more flowers
   the same way.
   Now you have five flowers.

5. Put the five stems into
   the hole of the spool.
   The spool is your vase.
   Now you have a
   vase of flowers.
   Give the vase of flowers
   to your mother or
   grandmother as a gift.

Toy Caterpillar

To make a toy caterpillar, you will need these things:

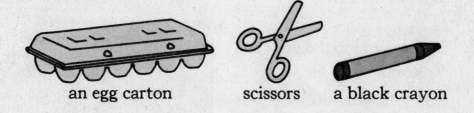

an egg carton   scissors   a black crayon

a very long pipe cleaner or two pipe cleaners
twisted together

After you have all these things, follow these steps:

1. With your scissors, cut out each
   egg cup from the egg carton.
   Now you have twelve egg cups.

2. Put the pipe cleaner through the center of one egg cup. Put the pipe cleaner through the center of the other egg cups. This is the caterpillar's body.

3. With your fingers, bend the pipe cleaner at each end.

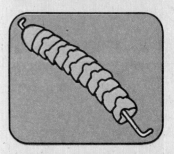

4. With your crayon, draw a face on the first egg cup. This will be the caterpillar's head.

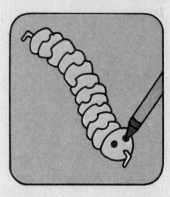

5. Your caterpillar is done. Have fun playing with it!

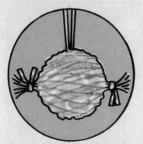

Bird Nesting Ball

To make a bird nesting ball, you will need these things:

plastic net tubing or bag that fresh vegetables come in

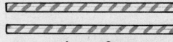

two twister fasteners

a piece of cord as long as your arm

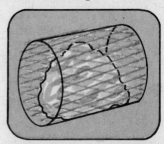

scraps of thread, yarn, string, and tissue

When you have all these things, follow these steps:

1. Put scraps of thread, yarn, string, and tissue inside the net tubing.

2. Close one end of the net tubing. Squeeze the net tubing together and put one twister around it. Twist it three times.

3. Close the other end of the
   net tubing.
   Squeeze the net tubing together
   and put the other twister
   around it.
   Twist it three times.

4. Put the cord through one piece
   of the net tubing.
   Tie the ends of the cord together.

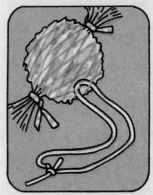

5. Your bird nesting ball is done.
   Hang it on a tree limb
   or in a bush.
   Birds will take the scraps of
   thread, yarn, string, and tissue.
   Birds use the scraps when
   building their nests.

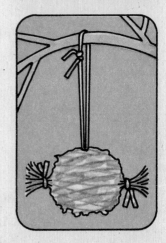

Angel

To make an angel, you will need these things:

a bathroom
paper tube

a lollipop in
its wrapper

blue poster
paint

a piece
of heavy
paper

glue

a white cupcake
liner

a paintbrush

scissors

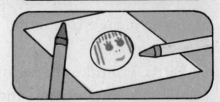
crayons

After you have all these things, follow these steps:

1. Put your tube on
   the heavy paper.
   With a crayon, draw
   around the tube.
   This is the angel's head.

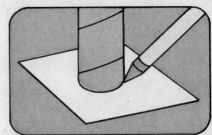

2. With your crayons, draw
   the angel's face and hair.

3. With your scissors, cut
   out the angel's face.

4. Put glue on the back
   of the angel's face.
   Put the angel's face
   on the lollipop's wrapper.

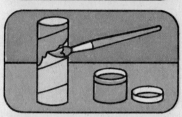

5. With your paintbrush,
   paint the tube blue.
   Let the paint dry.

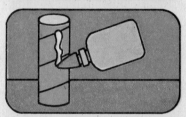

6. Put a line of glue halfway
   down the tube.

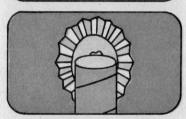

7. Put the bottom half of the
   cupcake liner on the glue.
   This is the angel's wings.

8. Put the lollipop in
   the top of the tube.
   Your angel is done.
   Your angel can be
   a party favor.
   She looks pretty beside
   the guest's plate, and
   she will taste good, too.

 # Picture Magnet

To make a picture magnet, you will need these things:

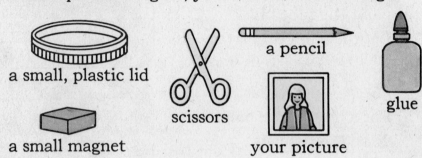

a small, plastic lid

scissors

a pencil

your picture

glue

a small magnet

When you have all these things, follow these steps:

1. Put the lid on your picture.
   Cover all of the face
   with the lid.
   With your pencil,
   draw around the lid.

2. With your scissors,
   cut out your picture.
   Cut on the line you drew.

3. Put glue all over the top
   of the lid.
   Put the back of the picture
   on the glue.
   Let the glue dry.

4. Turn the lid upside down.
   Put glue in the lid.

5. Put the magnet in the glue.
   Let the glue dry.

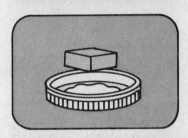

6. Your picture magnet is done.
   Write a note on paper.
   Put the note on
   the refrigerator door.
   Put your picture
   magnet on the note.
   Your picture magnet
   will hold the note
   on the door where it
   won't be forgotten.

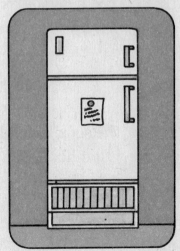

Toy for a Cat or Dog

To make a toy for a cat or dog, you will need these things:

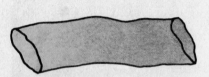

a piece of nylon hose
as long as your arm

a heavy sock

scissors

When you have all these things, follow these steps:

1. Roll the heavy sock
   into a ball.

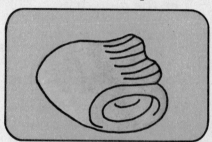

2. Put the sock ball inside
   the nylon hose.
   Put it in the center
   of the nylon hose.

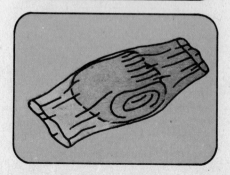

3. With your scissors, cut
    the nylon hose on one side
    of the ball.
    Cut it to where the ball is.
    Now there are two pieces
    of nylon hose.

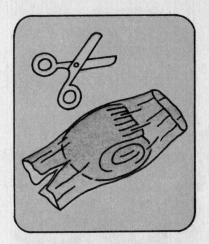

4. Tie the two pieces of
    nylon hose together.
    Tie two knots.

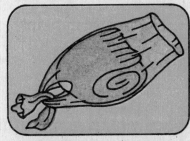

5. Cut the other side of the
    nylon hose the same way.
    Tie the two pieces together
    the same way.

6. The toy is done.
    Throw it for your cat
    or dog to chase.

Ghost

To make a ghost, you will need these things:

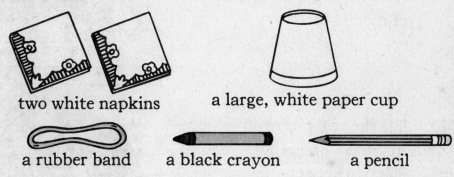

two white napkins   a large, white paper cup

a rubber band   a black crayon   a pencil

When you have these things, follow these steps:

1. Open one napkin.
    With your hand, roll the
    other napkin into a ball.
    Put the ball in the center
    of the open napkin.

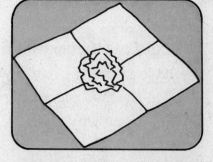

2. Put the eraser end of the
    pencil in the center
    of the napkin.

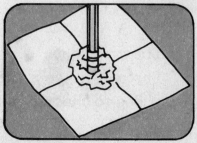

30